Anna Saunders

Feverfew

Indigo Dreams Publishing

First Edition: Feverfew
First published in Great Britain in 2021 by:
Indigo Dreams Publishing
24, Forest Houses
Cookworthy Moor
Halwill
Beaworthy
Devon
EX21 5UU

www.indigodreams.co.uk

ISBN 978-1-912876-26-6

British Library Cataloguing in Publication Data. A CIP record for this book can be obtained from the British Library.

Designed and typeset in Palatino Linotype by Indigo Dreams.
Cover design by Ronnie Goodyer at Indigo Dreams.
Printed and bound in Great Britain by 4edge Ltd.

Papers used by Indigo Dreams are recyclable products made from wood grown in sustainable forests following the guidance of the Forest Stewardship Council.

With love and gratitude to my mum Sheila Saunders
and sister Kate Saunders, for endless support and poetic
guidance, to Christine Whittemore for her intelligent and
encouraging editorial feedback, to my wonderful friends
and publishers Dawn and Ronnie for giving me the freedom
to write with fever and flames. Also to Howard and Marilyn
Timms, Zoe Brooks, Josephine Ley and Annie Ellis for their
friendship and inspiration.
And to other loved ones, mentioned in the poems,
but not named here.

Acknowledgements

With thanks to the editors of the following publications and on-line sites, where some of these poems have appeared: Anthropocene, As it Ought to Be, Burning House Press, Caduceus, Dear Reader, Dream Catcher, Envoi, Finished Creatures Magazine, Fresh Air, Good BAADPOETRY, Heron Clan magazine, I am not a silent poet, IceFloe Press, Inspired magazine, Ink Sweat &Tears, Nymphs Writing, Poetry Bus Magazine, Poetry Shed, Prole, Three Drops from the Cauldron, Vanguard Writes, words from the wild.

Also by Anna Saunders:

Ghosting for Beginners, IDP, 2018
Burne Jones and the Fox, IDP, 2016
Kissing the She Bear, Wild Conversations Press, 2015
Struck, Pindrop Press, 2014
Communion, Wild Conversations Press, 2010

CONTENTS

Feverfew

"Surely these white stars will heal?"

What I Learnt from the Owl

how to hunt in silken plumage
tooled up with talons and hooks

how to split the seam of the night
with saw-tooth wings

how to consume all I kill
yet stay hungry.

What I learnt from the owl

how to haunt sleep
my head – a phantom full moon

how to be outcast and avenger
spectre and seraphim, winged god and ghoul

bladed angel dropping from the sky.

What I learnt from the owl

how to voice my darkness
in hisses, in shrieks

how to drop from the heights,
heart-shaped face falling to earth

as if love itself were plummeting.

Time after Time the Same Bird is Born from the Flame

Here it comes, shedding embers as it struts

a feathered doppelganger of the last,
an identical gold-eyed genesis
scattering a surplus of silver plate from his claws
shaking down the same, ornate feathers of over-ripe hue
(deep as a peach skin gone to the bad).

Each day we pick at seeds and stringy meat
as the royal bird feasts on incense.

How did he earn the spokes of sun that ascend from his head,
the nimbus that blazes like a cloud backlit by the moon?

We ache for change, yet each creature that rules the court
is a rooster's brother with jaundiced eyes.

Not even death will bring an end to this.
The purpled bird stains the air
like dye bleeding through cotton.

Golden swan who entombed his father
in a burning planet,
emerged empowered.

How wrong we are to think that fire
can cauterise corruption.

Time after time the same bird is born from the flame.

We watch him rise on ash wings
singing as he buries the sun.

Now the Earth is an Embering Coal

Icarus didn't listen either
wasted the wings his father crafted
and when he hit the sun, the feathered sky wept.

Why did you demand to drive, Phaethon?
Your father offered you
any gift from the sky –
but still you wanted his cart.

What is it with you and Icarus?
His father warned that ascend too high
and the body, like a church candle
shrivels down to nothing.

Your father told you
keep your heart between earth and sky.

But carapaced in gold
hooved and pluming smoke
you seared the planet

just as if you'd taken a flame
to a scrap of paper
that the gods had tossed.

Now the earth is an embering coal
and your father's golden head is bowed in grief

as you plunge like a falling star
deep into the orphaned dark.

Hades Justifies His Off-Roader

Hades drives his huge cart, head held high.
He says he needs this tank
because down there
the lanes are sticky as treacle.

He wants bulk, and weight
as the wintered tides could wash a lighter chariot away.

Hades defends the emissions which plume
and unfurl like a scribble at the end
of a Death Warrant

fails to mention the cavernous boot,
black as a closed tomb
in which he will abduct a dozen Persephones.

Hades rides, his dark soul sealed
in a gleaming shell.

In Hades' cart he is raised above the creatures
that scutter below him, the terrified deer
that run from his wheels.

Who hears the kicks and whimpers
buried in the back of his cart ?

Not the winged martyrs that collide
with his windscreen

turned angelic white as they are picked out
in his headlights

before glistening like broken berries
when they hit the road.

The Wolf Speaks at the Tory Party Conference

We are tender to our own
and feed them our prey – pulverised
to a paste

a bloom of coruscating
scarlet, lumpen with gristle
on our lips.

We aren't how the novels portray us
we are worse than that.

You could say we cower from those
who are our equals

preferring instead to track down
the weak, the sick, the broken.

There we are half hidden
in the dark fir forest

panting, our lolling tongues
fat with want
glistening with cocoons of saliva.

Learn from us
seek out those you can overpower
break them down to that which your offspring can digest.

Reduce them to a quick
then let those from your blood-line
eat them from you.

The Benefit Minister's Mythological Creature of Choice

Once they had rested on a lonely shore,
the travellers laid out their food
bright fruits and berries, deep and red as the bruised lips
of the violently kissed,

plump and bold as pulvinated flesh,
largesse leaking a glitter and gleam onto stone.

How hungry they are, after weeks of travelling
how quickly the food is taken from their plates
as *The Benefit Minister* sweeps down
quick beak working deftly.

She doesn't choose to come back as a phoenix,
or Pegasus – foaled from Medusa
springing from a slashed mother's neck,
immortal winged horse
whose hooves could birth fountains.

She chooses a Harpy.

They are the Souls of the wind she says, an urge and energy
plucking the seas, forcing the grasses back in her direction.

She has forgotten they are beaked kleptomaniacs
carrying a stink of carrion.

Who we really are is occult and buried,
our egos are alchemists bedded down in the dark,
magicians – groping round to turn soiled sheets into doves.

She is half right about the word – she *has* harnessed the wind.

She rides the thermals
like a princess carried on a sedan chair.

Sisyphus in the Psychiatrist's chair

The Struggle alone to the heights is enough to fill a man's heart ~ Camus

It is a monstrous weight that pestles him down to a powder
yet Sisyphus won't let go of the rock.

The boulder is as smooth as a body eaten down
to the bone. Sharp as the edges of a skeleton,
yet it is his stone charge, given to him by the gods to shoulder.

As he lies on the couch his analyst reminds him he can
step to one side, let the hard orb hurtle.
But if Sisyphus lets go, his palms will hold only air.

Sisyphus weeps at the thought of losing the rock.

He remembers the hope he feels
when he thinks he may reach the heights

the exhilaration at the top of the hill
before he slides back down.

The Prosecution Build up a Case Against Jupiter

What did your attacker look like, Callisto?
'Like another woman, a golden-haired huntress, toes dusky and
dun with earth.'

And yours, Danae?
'He came upon me like a raining down of gold,
coins falling from a cloud,
dazzling, hard as shot, cold and glistening as hail.'

And describe yours Leda?
'A gold eye that never left me, wings – bulging like muscle,
a sharp piercing beak.'

Io, daughter of the river god?
'A dark cloud descending, a clammy moisture, shutting out the sun.'

Europa, what shape your abuser?
'Four legs and hooves, a wide back that I was thrown upon.'

No one has his name on their tongue.
Yet how similar were all the incidents.
His mark behind them all.

Deus pater, father god, living above the law,
thunder or eagle, severing
the air with beak and bolt.

Tearing the heart into pieces,
just like he cut up the realms of the sky.

The Husband's Net

Who could resist watching *War* seduce *Romance?*
Who wouldn't want to see battle grappling with desire,
Ares, wrestling Aphrodite, as if she were an enemy?

Their tryst has brought the peeping sun down from the sky,
its bald eye takes in every stroke, its gold mouth gobbles up
every kiss.

Her husband Hephaestus wasn't enough for her,
Aphrodite wanted Ares – insatiable,
man slaughtering, full of the fury of war.

Aphrodite desires a tempest
as the still boughs crave the hands of the storm,
the window hungers for pounding rain.

Yet jealousy creates the most intricate cage;
and how easily is lust ensnared –
the lovers are suspended in the husband's trap
dangled before the inhabitants of Olympus,
who deride them as they hang, entwined.

Look – their flesh bulges to pink globes
like ripe fruit in a net.

Yet Aphrodite doesn't care.

Suspended in an ambrosia of limbo,
airborne in a cocoon of desire

aren't we all impervious,
even to the mocking laughter of the gods?

Almost Eden

And they call the boy Pan meaning 'All '.

Our wintered love sought out a greening glade,
and there in the company of Dionysius
was the hollow-horned god of the pastures,
Lord of the Fields in an almost Eden.

We watched the grass grow rapidly at his hooves
heard a strange and fluting call in a slender throat.

What we did was unspeakable,
he was amorphous as Zeus
thunder bolt and bull then goat again.
My wife made shapes I'd never seen in our bed.

Afterwards he gnawed bark from a tree
crowed of tearing *Echo* into pieces,
how his pipes were fashioned from Syrinx, the nymph
turned first into reed then hacked down and pushed to his lips.

Despite, or perhaps because of this, we wanted him more.

It's not the same without him – we lie together stifling yawns.
I ache for his hoof when I reach for my wife's thigh.

When I hear the wind it reminds me of his piping
and how there was all of Eros in that song –
as if Syrinx herself, half flute, half woman

were singing of the terror and tenderness of love,
the exile and the home coming,
the adoration and damnation.

I seldom sleep.
My wife mutters to herself all night –
a single word refrain that sounds like *All, All.*

Two Seasons with Prometheus

In spring, like Prometheus
I stole fire and enflamed my lover's dark bed.

I carried it – a blazing creature
sprouting wings, gauzy feathers,
twitching as fast as a maniac's tongue.

That same season I saw the bird come,
its wing span a frayed shadow,
its cry harsh as the caw of the crow
tinged with the sweetness of the robin.

And the name of the bird was Love.

My soul – I was torn at by gold beaks,
The bird plucked my heart, as if it were tearing
ripe berries from a bush.

With time, my gouged heart healed.

That next summer I stole fire again.

Brought it to another lover like a spitting crown
like a seething, gold toothed mouth.

But the gods again bound me to rock,
cold spine of stone.

And the bird came back.

Wings like blades hacking up the sky,
its cry harsh as the caw of the crow.

On that first night they leapt into the mouth of the lion together

the papillae
of its scarlet tongue
grazed them

a rough weave
against bare skin.

They bristled
to a heat

plunged deeper
down its throat

became the lion's roar –
a fur throated velocity.

Alone, afterwards
she craves the gold thunder

still feels the hot barb
of tongue.

A Fire Art

A pyrotechnic prophecy – the fireworks you watched
in the middle of the day,

a foretelling of a combustion to come
a pre-playing, like a dream before sleep.

I imagined what you would have seen –

gold and silver blooms swelling in the sky
gilt-edged peonies, sparkling sea anemones,

glinting orbs opening and closing like mouths,
emitting a roar as they electrified the ether.

Later, in the dark alleys of the city
when the lamplight floods my face like moon glow
you turn to me – and ignite your gunpowder kiss.

Afterwards I remember how I had imagined *our* explosion
one morning, long before we set fire to the dark –

just if I had set off fireworks in the daytime
as a rehearsal for the main show at night.

Feverfew

That night the moon – a pearl bowl in the night sky
tipped a glitter into my upturned face
and I drank it deep.

Now I am drunk all day,
and this morning I plucked *febrifugia*,
to smother my flames.

Surely these white stars will heal?

Their heady scent fills my rooms, like an animal
moulting musky fur.

I dreamt I pushed my petals into your mouth
to soothe your throbbing head.

My realms are sky, the moon is mine.

I carry this lunar vessel,
cold but burning in my upturned palm –
a second offering to the gods.

What De Sade Says before Bringing Down His Arm

Lady, *Love* is fire speaking,
a burning plume that leaps and falls.
Its language is the lash.

My sweet, love isn't the lips landing lightly as a butterfly
upon a bush,
a gentle rosary played out in the bone beads of spine.
Love speaks in leather tongues.

How untouched you are, as yet,
your flesh white as a choir boy's eyes,
pure as a new communion dress.

Your skin's a blank page.
I'll inscribe it.

Looking for tenderness?
Seek agape, the brother love,
not Eros with its blades and barbs.

I gift you, my girl, the rapture;
pain's an ecstasy – Christ swooned upon the cross
his stigmata simple as stone
plain as full stops.

The marks I leave on you
are lavish as calligraphy.

My raging script unfurls across your back.
Stifle your sobs – they are censorship.

Each scream you issue
is an accolade to my searing art.

An Instrument

The flesh sings with kiss and punch
and hands inscribe their cursive symbols
in lash or stroke.

Hard to tell apart
an arm drawn back for a punch
and Cupid pulling his bow.

A woman plays Tchaikovsky
on pale, silken keys.

Her fingers descend with precise ferocity
forceful as palms pressed down
to resuscitate the heart.

Underneath his hands
I am a piano played in an empty church

suspecting the strings will snap
under the pounding of the hammers

imagining I need to be broken open
to release my song.

Leda, by the River

What was born of it was half holy
though it hurt

when the cumulus cloud of feather
came down, beaked and biting,
webbed feet like black fans slapping,
which of them was Leda, which was the swan?

So many sons and daughters of Cygnus
that first time they walked by the water

nestled heads forming hearts,
their roped necks arching like iced
bridges glinting with snow.

Countless swans reiterating the story
of the winged and rapacious lover,
one for each night they had perhaps.

The canopy
of silken white, the reaching beak – gold
and brutal, a sky-born ecstasy of pain.

The beating against their face,
the sky falling in feathers
as they offered themselves up to it again and again.

A Memory of Two Creatures Colliding

It's not as if we were together long, I tell my heart,
but it isn't listening.

In the flooded woods long blades of garlic
have been crushed by the storm
and water lilies float like white crowns
knocked from sunken kings.

A bough drips ivy and clings on to another tree trunk
like a drowning man grasping his rescuer's arm.

The pine tree is full of goldfinches, their metallic chatter
a teasing squabble. There is a dove, fluttering to a settle.

A male bird flies down and lands on its back.
There's a fury of pearl and platinum,
a flourish of wings like skirts billowing up.

The coupling is brief, but beautiful,
and in the spring light, the birds resemble angels.

I have all the symptoms of grief.
I am wide eyed at night, and my heart races.

But oh – the memory of two creatures colliding,
that airborne heat,
before both creatures flew off into separate skies.

The Delusion of Glass

Charles V – gone insane
after weeks of combat

felling friends and allies with a wild swing
of axe – afterwards running down the marbled corridors
screaming then sitting silently,
without moving, *so he won't shatter.*

Other cases, people with
The Glass Delusion – imagining themselves see-through forms,
susceptible to breaking.

At first, imagine how beautiful – your glaze
refracting light, all your tempests sealed like storms
in a paperweight, and feeling the rain roll off you.

Yet feeling fragile enough to split
at the lightest touch,
wrapping yourself in blankets so you won't smash
forbidding anyone to touch you or you will break to shards.

And being so glossy skinned
that a kiss leaves no sensation
just a mouth mark, a cloudy cherub bow

a wax stamp on a sealed letter, that no one
can ever open or read.

The Ghosts of Intimacy Fuck on my Bed

I walk into my room and see a pair of gauzy creatures,
airborne, balletic in their intercourse
stitched together and inseparable,
a wavering, seamless, line of gossamer.

A translucent man and a woman –
moving in synchronicity, like two damson flies mating
above a lake,

the Ghosts of Intimacy – fucking above my bed.

I stand there watching them, me, a woman
who has never shared her home, now cohabiting
with these amorous, entwined spectres.

I cannot take my eyes away as they hang in the air
like butterflies above a bloom.

I am thinking how they could not get any closer
when in a quick dart she slips into him,

slides under his tracing-paper skin, to be subsumed
into his heart as they soar above.

We do not get to choose what haunts us.
Here's my phantoms –
they have moved into my empty rooms.

I watch them disregard the solidity of my walls
as they flaunt how easily they become one.

I Stole a Butterfly

carried him home under my shirt, a second heart
fluttering.

In my dark rooms I stripped,
wore him as a plumy brooch against my bare breast.

I laid out every flower from which he could feed,
gave him ripe fruit so he guzzled and swooned

but when he flew towards the window and battered
against the glass I pulled down the blinds.

I couldn't blame him for wanting the wild flower meadows,
beauty draws its double

but I wanted him
with his mirrored wings, to reflect back only me.

He didn't last long without light.
I found him cold – wings flat as a fresh new page.

I scooped him up too easily, expected something more
than a gaudy fallen feather.

Who would have thought he would be so weightless
when dead?

No one told me quite how much he needed the sky.

I still feel that extra heartbeat, hard against my chest.

I am Feeding a Bird Called Love

I have read somewhere that it eats berries
so I scatter glistening orbs on the stone slab
of my window sill.

They are like beads from a broken necklace
the sun catches them and they blaze.
But it doesn't descend.

At night I dream of the beautiful night-sky wing.

I later learn
that the tease of my sweet morsels
won't satisfy it

that it prefers bodies flattened by collisions,
live flailing creatures
on their way down.

How bloodied is the lure
required to bring
Love down from the sky.

Forget the rosebud-red offerings
the pale breads.

Erotic Heaven wants the hot mess
the dripping bait.

Put out skin split from collisions
unspooling red ribbons,

the heart bulging and bruised to a pulp
like berries crushed underfoot for Love
to guzzle as wine.

I come back as a Horse

My owner leads me in from the cold.
His heating makes my flanks steam,
my breath plume and cloud. He shouts
as my skittering hooves crescent mark his shiny floor.

He has pictures of the races all over his wall
strained mares taking jumps
or being brushed down savagely
until their rumps blaze like precious stones.

I go straight from his rooms to the stalls.
We have to wear our harnesses all night.
It is compulsory and our necks burn.

Once I was there with just the moon for company,
its unblinking, blind white eye hung over me.

The names they give us are arbitrary and strange.
I am not mine. Nor is *Blue Nip,* or *Apollo.*

A young one never came back. If your legs buckle,
if your back is too weak, there's a bullet for you.

I love my mane, even when he winds it round his hand
to make a boxing glove.

All night in the stalls we whinny, and clatter.

I prefer to be out in the long grass, where crows
land lightly on my back and their fluttering feathers
blow the breeze onto me.

Once, a child passed me, said I had *kind eyes,*
felt pity for me.

I am pedigree I am snow fox I am Siamese

In the asylum they shave off my fur
so they can electric me.
When I mew they show me a clump
of blond in a flat palm and I say
I am pedigree I am snow fox I am Siamese.
At night the janitor creeps into the ward
where I sleep without blankets – tells me
I should be on all fours. I used to lie
in a man's lap, my belly rising and falling
like a swelling tide, my pink tips like
tiny gems, I'd try to sew myself
on him, my claws – glinting stitches.
When my warmth sent him under
I'd creep out into the dusk
bring back bloodied gifts
that I ripped down from the sky.
I brought a rat once, its entrails ribboning.
They say I have a severed self –
as if to love the warmth
of a soft cushioned room
and the spiked and musky dark equally
were an aberration. In the asylum
we are given cold meats.
I do not hunt because I am hungry.
He hit me when I brought the first mouse,
kicked me for the blackbird.
It's not out of love
that I lay these trophies at his feet,
but I let him think so.

Dearg-Due

She is a vampire

In this version, they lay stones on her newly-turned grave
heavy blue stones, slick with rain water
bulkier and harder than the human heart.

In this version, the girl who ended the sentence of her life suddenly
is given boulders as full stops and ballast, so in this version,

she does not rise and lies under earth like a wounded bird
matted feathers clotted against mulch.

In this version, her spirit does not fly in the night,
a gauzy ghost, a demon cooked up by trauma.

In this version, she does not seek retribution
for the blood leeched by her lover.

In this version, everyone is safe from her mouth.

In this version, everyone is still sleeping
and no lad feels the suction then bite
then emptying from his throat.

In this version, she was never hurt.

Or, at least, in this version,
they have lain stones over her body
so she cannot rise.

Night Crawler

What a smashed glass heaven
for her glossy body to break out into.

Her corrugate limb slithers,
her head emerges from black like Orpheus,
leaving her tail – like Persephone, below.

You call her *yeth worm, lob
night crawler, the intestines of the earth*
a *slithering nullity,*

you say that her love is just a slippery coupling
of two coiled crescents, slick against each other
like oily links on a chain.

Don't you know she turns the earth for you,
lets in air, angels?

The stars are too bright,
the earth is warm.

Down she goes to eat the dark –
Handmaiden of Hades, swallowing stones
like hard, grey truth.

Almost Raptors

I saw a heron – it crashed out of the bushes
as if breaking down a door with its head.

It looked more dragon than bird,
huge wings beating the skin of the sky.

Blackbirds on the lawn, goldfinches on the feeders
are what I am used to.

Birds that bite the husks off sunflower seeds
so they can eat the heart.
Pampered birds with beautiful songs.

These other creatures are taught by their wild fathers
that getting is brutal.

Last night, in a poor part of the city,
the words the poets uttered seem punched out
by the mic's clenched fist.

Pages flapping white,
words spearing our attention.

Back home, I read feather-light, fluttering poetry.

Did I tell you about the egret?
It shot out of the marshes, carried my startled, uttered *fuck*
to an unremitting sun.

Above the dunes, the marram grass sloughing
like a gasp
the bird's beak
opening and shutting in an urgent,
hard-won confession.

Last night, the poets, almost raptors,
split the air with their urgent flight.

Rare

*Raise me a dais of silk and down /Hang it with vair and purple dyes; Carve it
in doves and pomegranates/And peacocks with a hundred eyes.*
       A Birthday ~ Christina Rossetti.

The flesh is glistening to a blue
like the peacock behind her eyes magicked
by the Rossetti he recites.

The poem's bird is bejewelled with pomegranates –
rosy barbed fruits, Persephone's salvation, so she wouldn't starve.

As the lamb is served he recites the whole poem
and her mind deepens its hues.

For months their marriage has been a butcher's slab,
tenderising her.

The meat is almost opaque – a slender leaf of red,
a blood-stained diary.

Persephone paid a price for those sweet fruits.
Hades kept her in darkness for all the winters.

He kisses her tenderly on the lilac petal mark
on her wrist, she tries not to wince.
He says his love for her is *uncommon*.

Every mouthful tastes bloodied.
He explains to her that it is rare.
Fails to explain why it comes at such a cost.

Floundering

You are offering to lend me some money
when we see the young heron in the park.

From behind it resembles a sprouting bulb
with its long stem of neck.

It reminds me of the tulips dad planted
so we'd have colour after he had gone.

The heron sits on the rock in front of us,
and when a bulldog swaggers past,
paws scuffing the ground like knuckles,
you gasp.

Having no fear is dangerous round here
and the heron seems unsteady when it walks,
has no idea how to hunt.

It is perched on a lump of plastic
that it seems to have mistaken for a rock
and it belly flops into the water,
comes out empty mouthed.

We both know you can't make a living
from building poems. *That thing it's standing on isn't even real.*
You say.

Mum, you have your purse out again,
and that worried frown that dad used to have
when he was looking at the tulip bulbs,
wondering if they would come out in time.

On the Edge of Angelic

They were fluttering grey, half down, half feather,
and now are gone.

Who would prey on something so soft?
We can only speculate.

It wasn't a fox, though we have heard one marauding
through the streets at night, making the vixens scream.

The heron, omniscient god of the stump lake
hasn't taken them either.

The gust through the trees sounds soothing –
a hush to a crying child.

But how lethal the sharp blades of the iris leaves,
how vulnerable their exposed gold heads.

No one knows where the cygnets have gone.

Who would commit this crime when the victims
are on the brink of angel white?

Everything, a man tells me, *is sold on the dark web.*
You'd get a good price for young swans.

A robin is in reach. I could scoop it up, if I wanted to,
and at my feet – a blackbird.

I can almost pluck the gold ring from its eyes.

Torn

After the argument
we pull apart, ripping stitches.

My skin, shredded where the rough thread has torn
is susceptible to further fraying.

The beach is prairied, the marram grass
swarthy like the cack-handed craft
of a clumsy seam smith.

There's a cruel wind,
the lank cuffs of my shirt slap in the gust.

How do any of us,
split as we fall from heaven,
stay whole and airborne?

There's the answer –
in the low horizontal dart of the sparrow hawk

russet buffed bird
straight as a line of machined stitches
sewing the land to the sky.

So Many Storms Right Now

I blame you *Red Jasper* – small scarlet token
shiny blood boulder, impassioned stone.

I find you in my bed, bright on the sheets like lipstick
or menstrual flow, a broken rosebud calcified,
glossy as a lacquered box.

What a token you were for the weather gods!
They wore you in their hands like a blood blister
grasped you in their palms – warm as dice before the throw.

At your bidding the crops were quenched
gold ladders of hay rose to the clouds

the droughty cattle's thirst was slaked
and the grass sprung up, a green frenzy.

Red stone you are impervious,
as if laminated, and the rain runs off.

But what storm you have stirred
for the rest of us.

Too many tempests right now,
corroding the landmass,

pulling the flesh into a fury
like a house sucked into a seething sea.

Is this the ebb, or flow?

We are manacled in green
the grass like an anchor, holding us to the earth

new buds on the magnolias breaking through
as the blossom sheds itself like skin cells.

The moment is born, the moment dies, simultaneously.

How is it that late in life, even after losses,
the moment *sings*, symphonic.

Like the time we watched the song thrush
every speckle on its tiny chest as vivid
and electric as a mark by an Expressionist.

And then the blackbird, glossy and wet-ink black
pulling a worm out of the lawn
as if plucking a thread from the gleaming fabric of the day.

Sometimes the age feels apocalyptic
sometimes it feels as if we have just begun.

Like on that early autumn evening
when we stood with the waters around our toes
a warm, glinting baptism, engulfing us
and wondered, is the sea going out, or just coming in?

This wave,
these glinting luminous waters,
is this the ebb, or flow?

**For so long I have been wanting to write
about my mother's garden**

but halleluiah is hard, elegy is easier
and the poems keep chanting blue
yet when she tells me that the next time I visit
I can *help her buy a bird feeder*
all the gold and greens intone
immediately, and her spirit-
the lofty, lolling over foxgloves of it
the buttercup peppered lawn of it
the nettles, the *Nicotiana*, the single sunflower of it,
blossom and bloom and the page resonates
with a hymn of nettle leaf, poppy stalk, silken nap of rose
and I am there with her choosing a contraption for the birds
talking about how it will root into the earth
how it will reach, bough like, above the wall
so the cats can't paw down their prey
and how she will hang cylinders from it, like lanterns,
full of grain, and the goldfinches will come down
from the sky, yellow patched angels, eating the heart
of the seeds, and then, another leap forward
and here I am here writing this poem
singing halleluiah with the small choir of the heart
in the cool, white church that is this page.

The Air is a Chorus of Entreaties

Father, you have taught me that quiet can be a kind of poem
 ~ Devin Gael Kelly

Come here, come here, come here.

The beach is a prairie
and the soughing grasses sing.

The ponds are ink-dropped with tadpoles,
necklaced with long gleaming strings of eggs.

The rivulets are azure-skinned, sinuous brothers of the sky.

I am huddled in the dunes, reading the lines of an American poet.
The absence of his father echoes like wind in a tunnel.

People walk past with dogs,
walkers cling onto leads as if to their parents' hands.

I have you with me father, in the pause between thoughts,
in the solitude before another person walks in,
the blank space before I make these marks on the page.

The air is a chorus of entreaties
Come here, come here, come here.

So much Blood around my Name

You looked like an injured solider
after you had it done – clutching your arm
as if you'd taken a bullet.

How deeply I'd been etched into your skin,
you bloomed blood.

I didn't take yours, but instead read myself braille-like
through the plastic epidermis that covered the tattoo.

My name – spoken on your skin but silenced
by a translucent gag.

For months afterwards we needled each other,
until I left. Years later I hear about your death.

He couldn't go on without you. I am told.

I imagine your pale limbs under the earth.
Those four letters extinguished by the dark.

That morning, meeting you
under that azure sky,
the arching song of the blackbird
the scent of honeysuckle and fresh mown grass.

So early in the day and you were already wounded.

So much blood around my name.

The Sands are Golden Ghosts

After his death, there's no one out here except her
and the animal that has slipped its lead.

Starved of the sea, the ridged estuary beach
is an exposed ribcage,
the rack of something famished.

The tide turns, miles out,
a pale spine twisting.

Her dog circles a dead seal,
its skin leaking a glitter on to the shore.

Some bird of prey has plucked the pip
from the core

leaving an oval in its chest
perfect as Rembrandt's circle.

How immaculate is the hole left
when the heart is eaten out.

On the horizon the wind turbines turn acrobatic.
Moon-white crucifixes stripped of Christ.

Please step Aside So I can Write About the Living

You need to get the dead out of your poems

you told me but here I am writing of how
a month before you left this earth

we stood together in the gallery and I saw you reflected
in the fictive space of a painting

your form, gleaming white, translucent
as thin frost, or a sleek gauze

floating on the black glass as if airborne
a premature, amorphous haunting
your ghost getting here ahead of you.

You, see-through, overlaying an oil sky
which takes up almost all the canvas.

In that huge starless heaven,
a white dwelling is as diminished
as a tooth in a cavernous mouth,
a moth flying in space.

Your steps are so light
as you walk nearer to me.

How brave to paint so much darkness, you say.

It's a beautiful day to destroy love letters from a dead husband

so she carries a delicate bundle
of handwritten epistles into the garden.

When she tugs the ribbon they fall open,
and she pulls the stack apart and tears
the first letter down the middle.

The paper is beautiful, watermarked and thick.
His handwriting is delicate
as the brush work
on a Japanese water colour.

When the paper rips it sounds like a wasp
or a heavy sigh.

She could have destroyed them inside,
in her immaculate house which even now
smells of baking bread and furniture polish.

But perhaps
she wanted her daughters to hear the rip
so they would know what something coming apart
sounds like

and to see the ribbon, blue and lank on the grass
like a strip of fallen sky.

Silk Robe Spectres

I have been wearing the dead like hessian,
coarse rough cloths, my skin has been prickling with them.

I have been dressed in the dead as if in army uniform
buttoned up to the neck, constraining.

I have been wearing my lost like burel, burlap
like sisal fibre, their furze grazing my skin to a burn.

I have been dressed in the dead, like khaki
dun colours camouflaging me.

He tells me to wear my spectres like silk robes
the garb born of the Bombay Mori
of silver fish, lacewings, spiders.

To gown up in cocoons of larvae
wear my gone, my lost loves,
so I refract light.

He tells me to dress in the materials made by mayflies
that shimmer and dazzle and celebrate their brief day.

He tells me to luxuriate and gleam
in a gown that glints
then, like life, so easily and slickly slips off.

The Emergency Call

Are you in pain? Is your heart racing?
Do you see stars?
Are you panting as if you were walking home
and sensed something on your trail?
Are you breathing quickly like someone who has either
a – held the air in their lungs for too long – scared of losing it
b – been afraid to gulp in the ether in case it were contaminated
with fumes, broken promises, threats, or seductive words?
Is your head rotating like someone who has been used as a top,
a toy, or as a bottle spun to trigger a kiss?
Are you experiencing disequilibrium
as if you were on one foot, on the edge of a cliff
with the wild sea, or the barbarous city below,
crashing, crystalline, roaring from its depths?
Are you feeling wings beat frantically in your solar plexus?
Are you forgetting people's names, do you know what day it is?
Are you disorientated, struggling to find meaning?
Do you find it hard to get warm, even in a hot bath?
Do you ache to be held? Do you sometimes shape
a pair of arms from your pillows? Do you curl up foetal in sleep?
Does divinity escape you? Does God seem out of reach?
Would it be like catching steam in your hands
to experience the sublime?
Does your head throb?
Do you feel as if you have been hit hard over the head
with a brick?
Where else does it hurt?

Indigo Dreams Publishing Ltd
24, Forest Houses
Cookworthy Moor
Halwill
Beaworthy
Devon
EX21 5UU
www.indigodreams.co.uk